The Sh%t That Keeps Me Going

A humorous book on parenting.

Sheila Walls-Haynes

The Sh%t That Keeps Me Going

Copyright © 2016 by Sheila Walls-Haynes

ISBN-13:978-0692775097

Dedication

To my three crazy kids who have provided me with a lifetime of memories to keep me going.

and

To a good friend who inspired me by saying, "If anyone could pull this off, I believe you can."

Foreword

"Wow, this is such a great read!!!!!! While reading this I could picture everything. Since being a dad of three grown kids, two daughters and one son; I can relate in some ways and feel your joy and pain. Great job!"

Kent Murphy
Radio Personality
Murph in the Morning; ClassicSoul1075.com

Different Perspectives

Gazing out of the window is something we did often, just to see what was going on in the world around us. There are so many questions to be asked and so many discoveries that can be made just by looking out of a window.

I sat looking out of the window with my little pumpkin like we normally did every day. Suddenly with excitement he said, "Look mommy, a squirrel". I got a little excited too because we just learned what a squirrel was the day before, but when I looked I saw a cat. (Thinking to myself, 'Oh great, now we're going to call everything a squirrel'.) "No, that's a cat", I told him.

"But yesterday you said it was a squirrel."

"No honey, THAT'S a cat."

"And sometimes it's a squirrel?"

"No, it's ALWAYS a cat."

He looked up at me with that perplexed look of his, the one where his eyebrows kind of furrowed on his forehead. Just then I noticed the squirrel in the tree. With a little chuckle I said, "No honey, you're right. That is a squirrel." His little body relaxed as he gave a sigh of relief. I also breathed a sigh of relief because for a minute there I thought we were going to have problems.

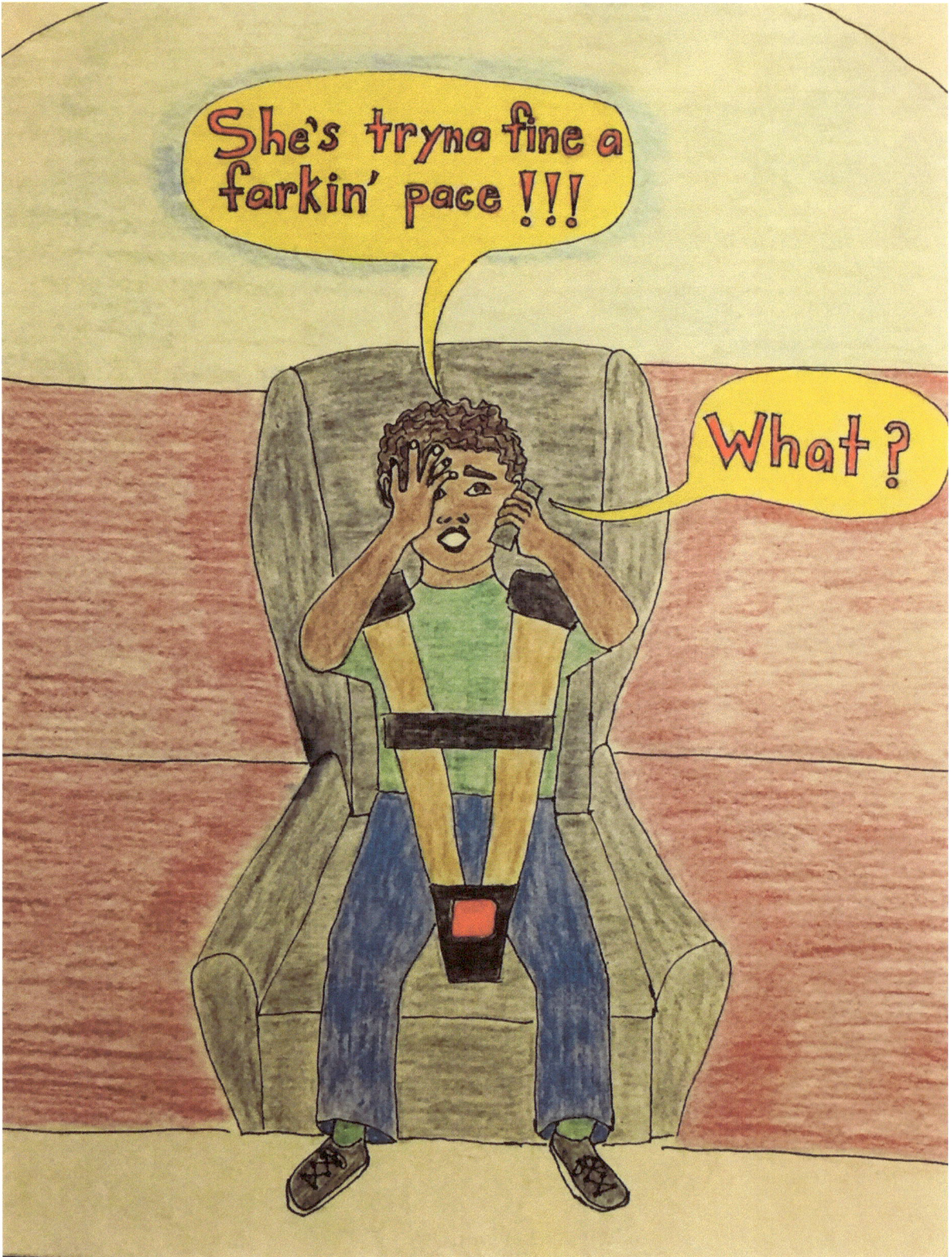

My Non-English Speaking Child

I speak English. That is to say, it's the only language that I speak fluently. When I say my youngest child didn't speak English, I don't mean that he was trying to speak another language, or even that he sounded like he was speaking another language. I only mean that when he first began to put sentences together in the only language that he had ever heard, a lot of times no one knew what the heck he was saying!

Picture this; I'm driving around, trying to find a parking space when my cell phone rings. I pass it to my youngest child who's sitting in his car seat in the back and I say, "Honey, can you answer that? Mommy's driving." He's really smart and already knew how to operate a cell phone.

"Hewoow", he says. I could hear the person on the other end saying, "What's your mommy doing?"

"She's farkin the car."

"What?"

"She's farkin the car!"

"What did you say?"

"SHE'S TRYNA FIND A FARKING PACE!"

By then the car IS parked and I take the phone from my verbally challenged little darling who is now very frustrated, only to hear the person on the other end say, "You'd better do something about your boy because he's cursing!"

Funky Him

I'll just say this, when a young child is innocent and gullible, it's a beautiful thing.

We're sitting at the computer and my then 2 ½ year old is trying to show me how to use a mouse by playing a game. He makes a mistake and says, "FUCK!" Now I'm thinking, 'Has this little boy lost his ever-loving-mind'? But what I say is, "Honey, you can't use that word".

To which he responds, "Yes I can".

"No baby, that word you CAN'T say".

"Yes I CAN".

(And now I'm thinking, 'Oh, I see what this is. This is turning into a battle of wills and you're not going to win little boy'.)

"Sweetie, that's a bad word and WE DON'T USE IT." Looking confused he said,

"My sisser sais it. Her sais it all the time. Her sais it yesterday. Her sais, fuck him."

"Well who was she talking to" I ask.

"Monique", he answered. Monique is one of my oldest daughter's friends and our next-door neighbor.

Thinking quickly I say, "Oh, you misunderstood. I know what they were talking about. See, there's this boy and he's really dirty and smelly. Funky is what people say sometimes when someone is stinky. That's what they were saying, funky him." Seemingly satisfied with that explanation, he says, "Oh", and goes back to playing his game on the computer. (And now in my head I'm thinking, 'SUCKER!')

Well Hell, He Must Be Crazy If He's Not Listening To Me

Now let me explain the 'Don't Turn A Corner Rule'. If you turn a corner, I won't be able to see you. If by chance some crazy person comes along and snatches you up and takes you away, I won't know where to look for you because I CAN'T SEE AROUND CORNERS!

My little guy and I were on our way to get his blood-work done to complete his yearly physical. Now keep in mind that he was deathly afraid of needles. As we approached the doctor's office, this little nut decided to take off running down the street. I didn't go after him because 1) I couldn't catch him and 2) he knew better than to step off the curb, cross the street or turn a corner. So what did he do when he got to the end of the block? That little runt turned the corner. As soon as he turned the corner, I went right into the doctor's office and asked for a referral for a psychiatric evaluation because he must have been crazy if he wasn't listening to me. But what I actually said to the doctor was that he was out of control. The doctor promptly wrote up the referral because she knew and trusted me.

The timing couldn't have been better. As soon as I stepped out of the doctor's office, with referral in hand, my little man was approaching. I snatched that little crazy man up by the collar and marched him straight to the hospital, which conveniently was only a block and a half away. We got inside and I picked up the phone in the lobby. A lady answered and I proceeded to tell her in the sweetest of voices, "My son is out of control and I have a referral to have him evaluated. Can someone please come down and talk with him?" She tartly responded, "Now Miss, it doesn't work like that. We would have to admit him in order to evaluate him." I asked the lady if she would hold on for one moment. Then I turned to my baby boy, still in my sweet voice and said, "Honey they said that you would have to spend the night here in order for them to find out why you're not listening and doing things like running off and turning corners. Do we really need to do this?" He started to sweat and fear enveloped him. His eyes were wide and he's looking at me like I was crazy because right then he KNEW FOR SURE THAT I WAS. "N-n-no mommy, we d-d-don't need to do this", he stammered. "I'll listen. I won't turn corners. I promise, I'll listen!" 'Aaah, sweet victory is mine', I thought to myself. I returned my attention to the woman on the other end of the phone, "I'm sorry to have bothered you. We won't be needing the evaluation at this time but thank you". Then to my son I said, "Come on honey, let's go home". I kept that referral on the ready for three years, when in actuality it expired after six months.

You Just Got Here

Some babies are oblivious to everything around them when they are born. They're just glad to be here, but my baby girl came into this world all knowing. Not only that, she had an opinion about things too.

My youngest daughter was a few weeks old when I called my husband and told him to bring home some diapers because I was about to put her last one on. A while later he called to say that he wanted me to jump in a cab and meet him at this camera shop on Grove St. I had been talking about getting a new camera because the one I had from my days as a photography major in high school had stopped working and it wasn't worth fixing. "But she has her last diaper on now and she just pooped so I HAVE to change her." He told me to figure something out and just hop in a cab. Just hop in a cab he said, as if that was a solution to my problem.

Well, figure something out is just what I did. I had purchased cloth diapers just in case she was allergic to the disposable ones. (Some babies are.) What I neglected to buy was those little plastic panties to go over them. Then a light bulb went off in my head and brought me a bright idea. I put on the cloth diaper and fashioned the little

plastic panty out of one of those black recycled plastic bags. This was back in 1994, when they just started making those recycled bags. They smelled like smoke and they were less pliable than regular plastic bags, so they made a loud crackly noise when you moved them around. Well, when I started to put that recycled-black-plastic-bag-panty on my baby girl, she turned her little head around and looked up at me as if to say, 'Oh hell no! I know this is NOT right!' To which I replied, "What do you know, you little twit? You just got here."

This so disproves what the pediatrician told me when I had my first child. I had a million questions about the correct way to do things and she said, "Don't worry so much. However you do it is fine because they don't know any other way." So much for that!

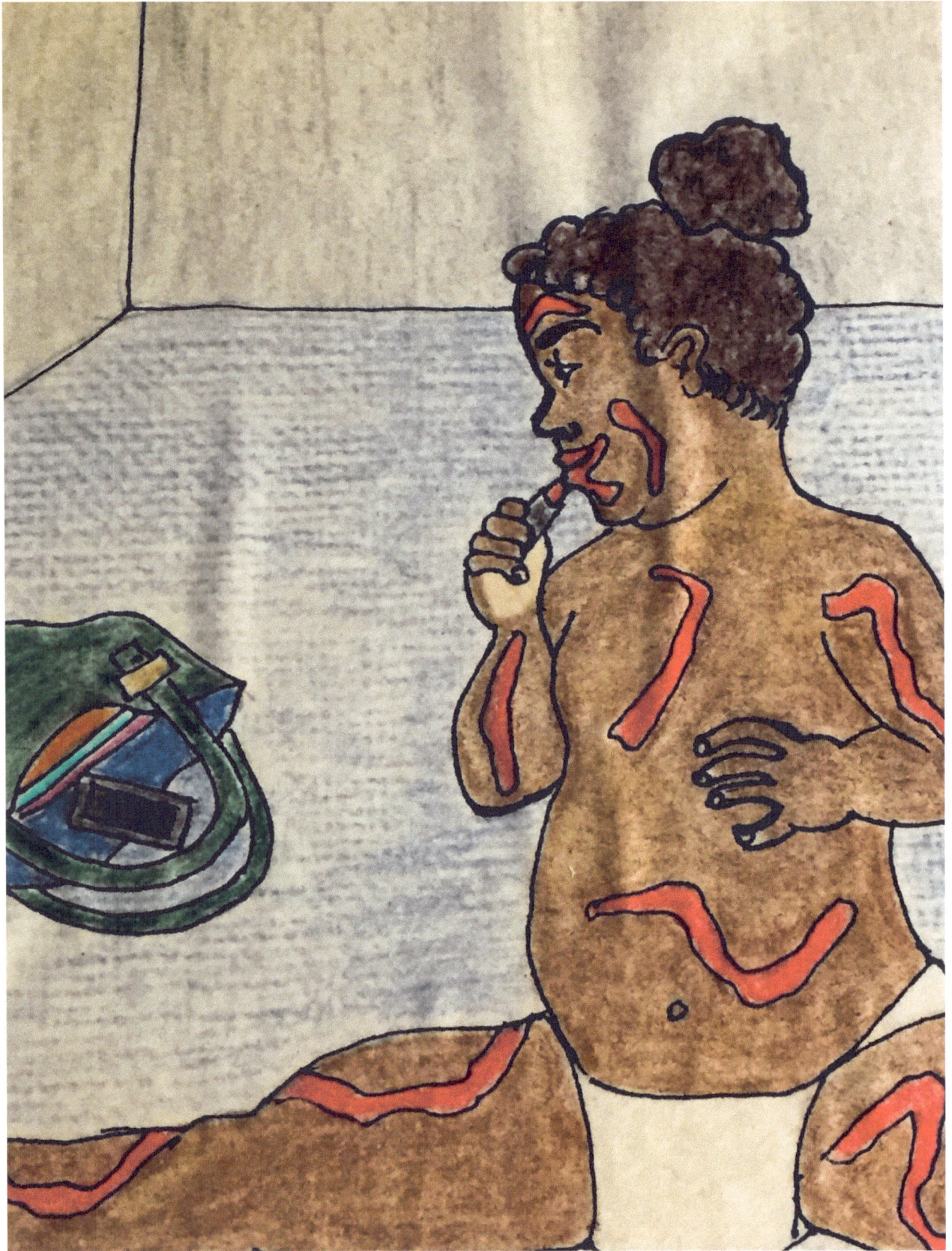

Hep Me, Hep Me

This brings to mind the old adage, 'Don't bite the hand that feeds you' and might I add, 'Don't ruin their very expensive lipstick either'.

I purchased my first MAC lipstick to attend a gala, a fundraiser for my oldest daughter's school. It was the most expensive lipstick that I owned and I had worn it exactly once. I'll never forget the color. It was called 'Fetish' and it was lovely. My baby-girl was about a year and a half at the time. She had been quite a daredevil so I'd taken the sides off of her crib when she was one because she used to climb out. I did this to protect her, to keep her from hurting herself. This left her free to wander around in the middle of the night… and she often did. About two weeks after the gala I felt a tapping on my leg in the middle of the night. Guess who it was? That's right, baby-girl and she was whispering something. "Do you want to get in the bed?, I asked.

"Nooooo", she answered and then I heard her say, "Mommy, hep me, hep me".

"Help you what?"

"Look", she said.

I couldn't see what she was talking about, so I turned on the light only to see her covered in 'Fetish' from head to toe. What I wanted to say was, 'You asked the wrong person for help because I am going to kill you', but what I said was, "Come on baby, let's go get cleaned up."

She Was A Foodie From Way Back

Some people eat to live. Some live to eat. While others don't need a reason, they just eat!

In August of 1995 we decided the family vacation would be a cruise to Bermuda. Looking back on it, I guess it wasn't such a good idea given that it was hurricane season and all. If I remember correctly it was Felix that was coming for us. Since Felix was hovering over the path to Bermuda, the ship's captain decided to go around him and take us to Nassau, Bahamas instead. This did not make me happy, AT ALL. I had friends that were traveling on another cruise ship bound for Bermuda and they got to go to Jamaica. I loved Jamaica. Why couldn't we have gone to Jamaica? Anyway, I digress. The first day of the cruise, we got to the cabin and there was chocolate on our pillows, which was nice, but not nice enough considering that I wasn't going to Bermuda. It was four days in before we realized that they left chocolates everyday. The reason for that being my little greedy-gut would dart into the room as soon as the cabin door was opened. She would bounce from bed to bed like a ping-pong ball. We all thought she just really liked the room but what she was actually doing was taking all the chocolates off the pillows, rolling herself into a little ball and stuffing them into her face.

The other thing we discovered about baby girl on this trip was that she was an incorrigible flirt. She'd unabashedly flirt with our waiter, Jerome, at every meal. At first I didn't get it. I mean, he was an okay looking guy; but nothing over the top, although he did have that cute French accent. Then I realized that he would cut up her food and feed her the first bite at every meal and she probably thought that batting her eyelashes got her the desired result, the food. What a little hussy. A smart one, but a hussy nonetheless. It was quite embarrassing, mostly because I didn't want people to think that she had gotten that kind of behavior from me. She didn't, of course. It just came naturally, which scared the heck out of me.

One of the few attractions on Nassau, at that time, was an ice cream shop. That being the case, there was always a long line, so I sent the hubby off to get ice cream for the family. It took him forty minutes, with us standing in the sweltering heat, AND he came back with FOUR CONES. What was he thinking? Baby-girl couldn't eat a cone. What made it even worse is that he handed her cone to her first, so I had no time to intervene. Her eyes got big and she clutched that cone like a miser holding on to gold coins. Even she knew it never should have happened. I was helpless, although dear old dad offered to take it away and get her a cup instead. That was EVEN MORE ridiculous than giving her a cone in the first place. So, we stood there and ate our cones and watched her eat hers, getting ice cream all over her face and in her hair, all the while laughing like a mad woman. Good job, Dad!

Talking Baby

Sometimes, when a child first starts putting sentences together, you just want to stick your fingers in your ears and say, 'lalalalalalalalalalalalala'.

It really makes you feel proud when you have a baby that's advanced. My first born rolled over at a month and a half. She said her first word at six months. She walked at ten and a half months. By the time she was one she was conversational. The only bad thing about that was that if she didn't remember exactly what something was called, she would call it something similar and that was good enough for her. The problem with that is that nobody knew what the heck she was talking about.

This brings me to the "present". You'll understand that in a bit.

I had gone back to work and put her in pre-school. She was learning all sorts of things. One day, with a puzzled look on her face, she asked me, "When did the present die?"

"Well gee honey, I'm not sure what you mean."

To that she said with a little bit of an attitude, "Was it like yesterday or something or was it a long time ago?" I stood there for a while trying to figure it out, not wanting her to get upset like she usually did when I didn't get what she was saying. I quietly said to myself, "the present, the present", as if repeating the words would help me figure it out.

She heard me and shouted, "You know, you know, like GEORGE WASHTISHUN."

"Oh that! That was a long time ago, honey." Kids should come with an interpreter.

Thank You, Mommy

Sometimes all it takes is a simple thing like sincere gratitude to melt your heart.

Let me start off by telling you that by the time my first-born daughter was three, her hair was down to her butt and thick. For every strand of my hair, she must have had 10. That meant that it was an all day job just to wash it, blow dry it, part it and put it in two cornrows. That being said, I'm sure you can understand why I initially said 'no' when she asked if she could get wet outside with her new found friends. The neighbor on the first floor had run a hose from his house to the terrace and had connected a sprinkler to the end. We had just moved to the neighborhood and she was fitting in pretty well with everyone. She even made friends with 'Vinnie', the mailman. The neighborhood kind of reminded me of how it was when I was coming up. All the kids on the block played together. All the activities were huge because you had fifteen to twenty kids participating in them. Those activities also included her inviting all those little rug-rats to my house for lunch, EVERY DAY. (Something I had to put a stop to pretty quickly).

As I watched my little girl looking out of the window, seeing her friends having fun and hearing them yell, scream and giggle, I began to feel a little guilty.

Then I remembered the dreaded SWIM CAP she'd always refused to wear but I figured it was worth a try, so I offered it up. "Honey, if you wear the swim cap I'll let you get wet."

To my surprise, she responded with, "REALLY? OK mommy!" She quickly ran and changed into her bathing suit, threw on a pair of shorts and we stuffed her hair into that swim cap. Then she sprinted to the door, flung it open and darted out. It really was enough for me just to see how happy she was, but just before the door closed, she popped her head back in and with the biggest grin on her face, she gave me the most sincere, "Thank you, Mommy". I was over the moon.

Not So Sweet Sixteen

Sometimes all you need to do is just listen to your mother (or NOT).

For the most part, my oldest daughter was a pretty good girl. She was 15 when she first blatantly defied me. I'll never forget. It was September 11, 2001. She had spent the night at a friend's house in Hoboken. I was trying to convince her to take the Path train in to school because I didn't want her to be late. You see, it ran more frequently than the bus. She wanted to take the bus because it would leave her closer to her school and she wouldn't have to take the subway. We went back and forth about it for a while when she suddenly said, "I'm not taking the PATH!", and promptly hung the phone up. I looked at the phone for about three seconds and decided against calling her back because I still had to take her sister to school. I would ring her little neck when she got home. That morning the Twin Towers were hit. The tunnels of the Path that lead from Hoboken to the World Trade Center had cracked. She would have been on one of those trains that got trapped in the tunnel or in the Trade Center itself. I was so grateful that she didn't listen to me.

Fast-forward a year, and we have an out of control sixteen year old. Sixteen is theat magical age where kids think they're grown. Her Jersey friends had their

driver's licenses and she was going to parties out of state. She was hanging out with a wilder artistic crowd but worst of all, she was telling me that she NO LONGER WANTED TO PLAY THE VIOLIN. She had been playing the violin since she was three. People cried when they heard her play, not because it hurt their ears but because it was so beautiful.

One day Brenda, her selfless violin teacher, brought her all the way home and came upstairs. This was a little unusual, but I always enjoyed her company so I was glad to see her. She gave my rebel a cold stare and told her to show me her violin. She opened the case and the violin was in pieces. The story I got from my teen was that it slipped out of her hand and fell down a flight of stairs. When she left the room Brenda said, "Look at that violin. I can tell you that THAT WAS NO ACCIDENT! She wants to quit but don't let her". Brenda told me that her own daughter had tried the same thing and she didn't let her quit either. I listened to her because after all, she wasn't even charging me for the lessons so she had nothing to gain. Much to my darling's disappointment, we made arrangements to get her another violin. The lessons only lasted about another four to six months; something she now regrets, and somehow she manages to blame me for. I have to tell you though, every now and then an image of her smashing that violin like a rock star crosses my mind and I crack up.

So you see, although my life hasn't always been easy and at times it's seemed unbearable, being able to live in the moment and find humor in things helps. The memories I have of my crazy kids make me chuckle and sometimes double over with laughter. When times get tough, that's definitely The Sh%t That Keeps Me Going.

www.ingramcontent.com/pod-product-compliance
Lightning Source LLC
Chambersburg PA
CBHW061059090426
42742CB00002B/92